7 Habits of Highly Effective Church Members

Christians, Ministers, Elders and Deacons

7 Habits of Highly Effective Church Members

Christians, Ministers, Elders and Deacons

Mike Mazzalongo

BIBLETALK.TV

ISBN-10: 099041552X
ISBN-13: 978-0-9904155-2-7

BibleTalk Books
14998 E. Reno
Choctaw, Oklahoma 73020

Scripture quotations taken from the New American Standard Bible®,
Copyright © 1960, 1962, 1963, 1968, 1971, 1972, 1973, 1975, 1977, 1995
by The Lockman Foundation Used by permission. (www.Lockman.org)

TABLE OF CONTENTS

7 HABITS OF HIGHLY EFFECTIVE
CHRISTIANS

The idea for the title and approach of this book comes from Steven Covey's popular book entitled, "The Seven Habits of Highly Effective People." I will talk a little more about this further on in the book but suffice to say that Mr. Covey's research found that highly effective and thus successful people who made an impact in their various fields shared a specific set of character traits and habits which he analyzed and summarized in seven categories.

I believe that the same case can be made for the church and those who play different roles in the church. From the saints in the pew to the ministers in the pulpit, from those who have special responsibilities to those who are responsible for the overall leadership. There are characteristics and habits that distinguish those who are effective and successful in their personal walk with Jesus as Christians, as well as those who serve as preachers, deacons and elders.

As Christians, we all need to examine ourselves in order to carry out a more dynamic ministry to one another and the community. I think it is important to have a clear standard to strive for and to measure ourselves against as we serve the cause of Christ in the various roles we have been given by the Spirit.

Please know that all of you will have some of these habits developed to various degrees depending on your maturity, knowledge and commitment. Please realize also that none of us will have all of these habits perfectly developed. What I am giving you is the ideal to shoot for and a template to copy in your striving to grow as Christians at every level of maturity and responsibility.

Remember, the title of the series emphasizes the fact that Christians at every stage have certain habits that enable them to be effective and thus successful. So, if we parse the title, we have two key words:

HABITS – These are actions that are engrained, that have become natural because of continued repetition. They are the things we do without thinking but accomplish with skill and precision.

EFFECTIVE – This word refers to the quality of our lives and our service. People can be Christians, deacons, preachers and elders in name and in title. But to be effective as disciples of Jesus, or effective as His ministers, elders or deacons, means that we produce fruit in our personal spiritual lives as well as our particular ministries. A person can wear a title without actually being effective.

This book, therefore, will describe the habits cultivated and engrained in those who actually are effective as Christians and as Christian leaders, something I hope all of you will begin to strive for from this day forward.

We know that Christians do not simply come out of the waters of baptism and immediately become effective saints. We observe that through practice and discipline in the Holy Spirit they cultivate habits that become a natural part of their lives and eventually enable them to become more effective as Christians in the service of the Lord and His church. There are many, but I have chosen seven common habits of highly effective Christians that I have read about in the Scriptures and seen over the last thirty-five years in brothers and sisters who have had great success as disciples of Christ.

Habit #1 – Effective Christians Read and Obey God's Word

Effective Christians are effective because their lives are powered by the Word of God. They know what God says and that knowledge empowers them to make right choices in more consistent ways. They resist temptation because they have God's Word on their hearts and on their minds. They are more able to stand up for right, give right advice, say the right thing at the right time because they know what right is, they can even quote it.

Paul congratulates Timothy in II Timothy 3:15 because he knew the Holy Writings from an early age, and this knowledge led him to salvation. But this knowledge also led Timothy into his vocation as an evangelist, as a partner with Paul in missions and as an example of effective Christianity for all future generations.

You cannot be very effective as a Christian (in preserving your faith or sharing it with others) if you do not know and obey the Word and you cannot know it if you do not read it. Effective Christians begin to pull away from immaturity and entanglement with sin and the world to the degree that they develop the #1 habit of reading the Bible on a regular basis.

Habit #2 – Effective Christians Have an Active Prayer Life

We cannot effectively experience the life of Christ unless we read about it in God's Word. God cannot effectively change, shape and mold our lives unless we share it with Him in prayer. Look at those people in the New Testament that God used in a mighty way, were they not men and women of prayer? Jesus prayed at every step of His ministry. John the Apostle was in prayer when he had the vision to write the book of *Revelation*. Paul prayed constantly for direction in his ministry. Lydia was at a prayer meeting when converted. (Acts 16:13-15)

The habit of prayer is what keeps us tuned in to God and sensitive to the Spirit. Without the habit of prayer the noisy demands of the world and the impulses of our flesh are all we can ever hear. The effective Christian succeeds in keeping the faith and growing in faith because he stays in touch with the Spirit of God through prayer.

Habit #3 – Effective Christians Set "Spiritual" Goals

There is a saying in business, "If you don't plan for success, you are planning to fail." Whether it is a business or a school, a family or a sports team, everyone needs to plan ahead. What makes us think it is any different for our spiritual lives? Effective Christianity requires that we set personal spiritual goals and actively work towards them, making the necessary sacrifices to eventually reach them. No gold medalist at the Olympics ever stood on the winner's podium without having made a decision to pursue a personal goal long before. No politician ever won an election without setting this victory as part of his or her career strategy.

So whether it is to be more faithful to services, or starting to help out in some way; a commitment to changing a bad habit for a good one, or doing a better job in what we have already been given to do... We do not become more effective as Christians unless we visualize a realistic goal, strategize a way of achieving it and commit ourselves to reaching it in a certain time frame with help from God through faith in Christ.

Paul the Apostle saw and heard Jesus, could perform miracles, established the church in the Roman Empire, but he was continually setting new goals for himself (to go East to Asia, to evangelize Spain) in order to widen his vision for the future and keep his spiritual adrenaline pumping.

Habit #4 – Effective Christians Cultivate Talents of Others

I don't know where I would be without Jim Meador, Hemzie Brown, Charles Branch, Stafford North, Louis Thompson, Edsel Hughes to name a few... These are all people who at one time or another in my Christian life helped me to grow spiritually. Each of these were effective Christians who took the time to help cultivate different aspects of my Christian walk and ministry. They were my mentors at various stages of my development. Jim taught me how to study the Word. Emmie encouraged me to preach. Charles made it possible for me to get training. Louis showed me how to do local work and Edsel's encouragement gave me the strength to pull up roots and move my family to a place where I knew no one. Part of their effectiveness was helping me to become more effective as a Christian and then as a minister.

Barnabas was one of those people in the Bible who so clearly demonstrated this habit, starting with Paul as a new convert and later continuing with Mark the young missionary.

Effective Christians realize early on that in order to stay effective they need to build up others in the body.

Solomon says:

> "As iron sharpens iron, so one man sharpens another."
>
> - Proverbs 27:17

Paul says it in another way:

> "...we are to grow up in all aspects into Him, who is the head, even Christ, from whom the whole body, being fitted and held together by that which every joint supplies, according to the proper working of each individual part, causes the growth of the body for the building up of itself in love."
>
> - Ephesians 4:15

Note that the body builds itself up. When I build you, I also build me. Effective Christians are easy to spot, they are the ones **asking** for volunteers.

Habit #5 – Effective Christians Take Responsibility for Souls

Paul says to the Philippians in chapter 2, verse 12 of their letter,

> "...work out your salvation with fear and trembling." And it was said of the Bereans that they, "... (examined) the Scriptures daily."

The Bereans did so to verify if Paul's preaching was accurate according to God's Word. Highly effective Christians take responsibility for their own souls and the souls of others, especially the lost. They are effective because they know that Christianity is not a game and faith is not a crutch for the weak. Effective Christians make a difference in their congregations and in the world because they understand that the stakes are very high (eternal life) and the enemy is very dangerous (Satan).

Harry Truman, the former President of the United States, was very popular as a tough minded, no-nonsense leader. He had a sign on his desk that said, "The Buck Stops Here." This meant that he was the President, he was responsible, and he knew it.

We are each responsible for our souls (not the preacher, not the elders), in the end we will be judged on what we said and did (II Corinthians 5:10). Effective Christians know this and do not waste their time or spiritual energy on things that would endanger this most precious possession. They have the habit of putting what is good for souls first. This is why these brethren are so interested in saving souls, why they are good at it, why they work hard in evangelism and visitation: they know the value of a human soul. Think back to the one who brought you to Christ or brought you back to Christ... I am sure that that brother or sister fit very well my profile of the effective Christian.

Habit #6 – Effective Christians Serve Others

Jesus said:

> "…the Son of Man did not come to be served, but to serve…"
>
> - Matthew 20:28

Do you think any of us would be here if Christ came as a royal king with attendants receiving the service He actually deserved? No, we are here with a hope of heaven today because Jesus Christ *"emptied Himself,"* as Paul says in Philippians 2:7, *"…taking the form of a bond servant."* What saved us was His very effective service on the bloody cross of Calvary. What continues the salvation He delivered once for all is the effective service of millions of men and women who give themselves in service to reach each new generation of souls who are lost without Christ.

Effective Christians have cultivated the character of Christ within themselves by cultivating His character of selfless service to others for their good, their advantage and their salvation. For effective Christians, service is not an inconvenience they must bear in order to avoid guilt. No, like Epaphroditus, service is a way of life born out of love for Jesus.

Habit #7 – Effective Christians Remain Focused on the Kingdom

More Christians lose their way because they just do not pay attention! In the parable of the sower and the seed, Jesus describes the person who receives the Word and grows for a time but the worry of the world and the deceitfulness of riches chokes the Word and stops his growth (Matthew 13:23). Note that the man was not a great sinner, he did believe, he did practice his faith, he grew! What destroyed his soul were the things we all face each day as Christians: the things that do not seem dangerous: worry about deadlines, debts, health, family, busy-ness, activities, emergencies, making it, looking good, keeping up. He became focused on these things and these things drew his attention, his energy and eventually his soul into their orbit.

Effective Christians have learned to keep the kingdom first and have not allowed the "cares" and the "desire for riches" overwhelm their spiritual lives. When they do, they are quick to repent and refocus their attention to where it needs to be. As a matter of fact, effective Christians continue to increase their involvement, their love, their very lives in the affairs of the kingdom and decrease their involvement, their love and their lives in the world. Effective Christians know that the kingdom is forever, is reality, is life itself, and the world is temporary, is sinful and full of death. They know this and live accordingly.

Summary

Well, there you have them, 7 habits of highly effective Christians. There are Christians who have managed to cultivate a lifestyle that incorporates these habits. In other words, practicing these habits has created a certain Christian character and ability that makes these women and men highly effective as disciples of Christ. If you are a new Christian wondering "where do I go from here," or if you are an experienced Christian wanting to go to a higher level, then pursuing these 7 habits will provide direction to more effective Christian living and service.

Once again, to become more effective as Christians, you need to develop the habits of:

- Reading your Bible regularly
- Praying to God daily
- Setting personal spiritual goals
- Cultivating your abilities and the abilities of others
- Taking responsibility for your soul and then the souls of the ones who are weak or lost
- Stepping up your rate and intensity of service
- Remain focused on spiritual instead of worldly things

Of course, all of this is for those who want to become effective as Christians as opposed to those who simply want to affect a Christian pose.

For some, there is no spiritual effectiveness possible because there is no Spirit within them. They have not yet obeyed the Spirit's initial command to repent and be baptized in order to be forgiven of sin and wear the name and person of Christ.

For the brethren, I hope you will see more clearly the narrow path before you in Christ that leads to effective, joyful, spirit-filled living, powered by the cultivation of these habits.

God bless you as you grow to become highly effective Christians.

7 HABITS OF HIGHLY EFFECTIVE
MINISTERS AND ELDERS

The title of this book is based on a book by Steven Covey entitled, "7 Habits of Highly Effective People." In his book, Mr. Covey reviewed two hundred years of "success type" literature and found that regardless of their age, culture or profession, effective and thus successful people shared a number of common character traits which he reduced to seven for his book.

I have used the same approach using the Bible and my experience in church work over the years to identify the seven most common characteristics of effective Christians. In this chapter we continue this study by listing the seven habits of effective preachers and elders.

3 Habits of Effective Preachers / Ministers

We begin with the habits of effective preachers; there are many but I will name three very important ones. Now I must repeat that what we are searching to do for all Christians whether they are deacons, preachers, elders or saints without a particular leadership role, is to describe those common habits that make these people effective.

As I have said, there are many who call themselves Christians, many who have been appointed as deacons and elders, many who have been commended to the ministry of preaching, but are not effective in these roles! If just wearing the title preacher made one effective then a church could randomly select any preacher to serve them as minister. But churches do not do that because they know from experience that not all preachers are equally effective and some are not effective at all.

In this chapter we are defining the habits that effective preachers and elders must cultivated in order to become successful at what they do. As far as preachers are concerned, there are 3 main habits or characteristics that identify the truly effective minister. These are described by Paul in his letter to a young evangelist named Timothy in II Timothy.

Habit #1 – Effective Preachers Purify Themselves

> For this reason I remind you to kindle afresh the gift of God which is in you through the laying on of my hands.
>
> - II Timothy 1:6

Timothy was holding back in his ministry because of his youth and the presence of many distractions in the world. He was also timid because of the fear of persecution by the Jews and certainly by the Romans. Paul encourages him to renew his gift and purify himself continually by separating himself from those things that would hinder, distract or slow him down.

Even preachers get into a rut: it could be a rut of fatigue, of boredom, of laziness or sinfulness. It is usually a rut where the preacher starts majoring in minors to avoid the true and hard work of ministry. Effective preachers have the habit of purifying themselves on an ongoing basis in order to remain fresh, open and sensitive to the Spirit's lead.

Effective preachers cultivate spiritual habits that serve to purify their minds and hearts continually:

- They read the Bible continually and not just for sermon prep.

- They make time for personal prayer aside from prayer during public worship.

- They read and study material that will expand their minds and ministries.

- They cultivate relationships that keep them accountable because every minister needs someone, aside from his wife, who will tell him when he is wrong.

- They are involved in activities that serve the brotherhood in general and not just the local church. This serves to expand their view of the kingdom.

- They do what is difficult first. I once knew a preacher who hated to study and prepare lessons but loved computer work. He would spend 3 days getting the bulletin ready, preparing mission reports with statistic sheets, graphs, etc. He would run errands and tend to the office. Finally, on Saturday night, he would get his lesson together and Sunday morning it would show!

Effective preachers continually purify themselves and their ministries in order to maintain the enthusiasm and passion that characterized their original call to minister.

Habit #2 – Effective Preachers Preach

> Therefore do not be ashamed of the testimony of our Lord or of me His prisoner, but join with *me* in suffering for the gospel according to the power of God, who has saved us and called us with a holy calling, not according to our works, but according to His own purpose and grace which was granted us in Christ Jesus from all eternity, but now has been revealed by the appearing of our Savior Christ Jesus, who abolished death and brought life and immortality to light through the gospel, for which I was appointed a preacher and an apostle and a teacher. For this reason I also suffer these things, but I am not ashamed; for I know whom I have believed and I am convinced that He is able to guard what I have entrusted to Him until that day.
>
> - II Timothy 1:8-12

Paul is still passionate about the gospel, even when he refers to it in a letter to a fellow believer and worker. Despite the fact that he has suffered for the gospel, he is still completely convinced and fully engaged in the spread of the Good News.

Effective preachers are effective because they are excited by the message, not where they will preach the message or how many people will be there. Paul is zealous and he is simply writing to one person! What makes preachers effective is that they want to preach in season or out, big crowd or small, friendly hearers or skeptical ones, local or international, in person, on TV, radio, print, or the internet. They just want to preach!

Effective preachers are convinced that the gospel is God's truth to man and they are anxious, even uncomfortable if they do not preach.

Habit #3 – Effective Preachers Persevere

When I say persevere, I mean that preachers who succeed in ministry are those who are able to "keep on keeping on" they "last" they "hang in there" they have a persevering spirit.

In his letter to Timothy, Paul encourages him to persevere in 3 areas:

A. Persevere in Doctrine

> Retain the standard of sound words which you have heard from me, in the faith and love which are in Christ Jesus. Guard, through the Holy Spirit who dwells in us, the treasure which has been entrusted to *you*.
>
> - II Timothy 1:13-14

> You therefore, my son, be strong in the grace that is in Christ Jesus. The things which you have heard from me in the presence of many witnesses, entrust these to faithful men who will be able to teach others also.
>
> - II Timothy 2:1-2

Persevering in doctrine or teaching means to continue diligently teaching God's Word even when it is inconvenient, or when people will not listen or obey. It also means to persevere when there is opposition from those in and out of the church. Finally, perseverance requires one to confront those who are in error and train others in the proper teaching of the Word.

The preachers' job is to minister the Word in every circumstance and successful, effective preachers make sure they do not get away from that primary task in their many sided job.

B. Persevere in Ministry

> Suffer hardship with *me*, as a good soldier of Christ Jesus. No soldier in active service entangles himself in the affairs of everyday life, so that he may please the one who enlisted him as a soldier. Also if anyone competes as an athlete, he does not win the prize unless he competes according to the rules. The hard-working farmer ought to be the first to receive his share of the crops. Consider what I say, for the Lord will give you understanding in everything.

Remember Jesus Christ, risen from the dead, descendant of David, according to my gospel, for which I suffer hardship even to imprisonment as a criminal; but the word of God is not imprisoned. For this reason I endure all things for the sake of those who are chosen, so that they also may obtain the salvation which is in Christ Jesus *and* with *it* eternal glory. It is a trustworthy statement:

For if we died with Him, we will also live with Him;
If we endure, we will also reign with Him;
If we deny Him, He also will deny us;
If we are faithless, He remains faithful, for He cannot deny Himself.

- II Timothy 2:3-13

In other words there are many distractions and temptations in the world and ministers need to be careful not to become trapped in these. Some ministries are ruined by worry or sinfulness because the preacher becomes more involved with something other than ministry and this thing leads him to ruin. Successful, effective preachers keep their eye on the prize and their hands on the wheel of ministry without detours. I have been offered partnerships in many ventures but always refused because it would be a distraction. I don't want to be concerned about anything other than my family and my ministry.

C. Persevere in Love of the Church

There are many more comments by Paul to Timothy in both his letters about being a good preacher. Suffice to say that the most effective preachers I have met and seen are those who love the Lord's church. No matter how they are treated; whether they have preached in big or small churches; in the Bible-belt or in the mission field; they continue to love the Lord's church and sacrifice themselves for it.

No matter how much education you have or how skilled a speaker you are, if you don't love the church you cannot be effective as a minister. People can sense this and will respond to you accordingly.

Summary I

There are many who wear the name minister/preacher. Colleges and preacher training schools are producing a new crop every year. But effective preachers achieve success because they have cultivated 3 important habits:

1. They continually purify themselves through prayer and reading the cleansing Word of God.

2. They continually preach the gospel with enthusiasm and avoid debates over issues, personalities.

3. They continually persevere in teaching the Word to others, service to others and promoting the church of Christ to the world.

This is what they are about, this is what is central about them. If the only thing that you remember about the preacher is his hobby or his passion for football, something is wrong! Of course there are many other factors that contribute to successful ministry. Things like people skills and getting in touch with the culture of the people you are preaching to; however, without the habits I have just spoken of, a man will not become effective in ministry no matter how many friends he has in the church or how well he fits in to the local scene.

4 Habits of Highly Effective Elders

It is difficult to say all that needs to be said about the role of elders, so I will have to summarize and compress my comments into 4 key habits for effective eldering.

Habit #1 – Effective Elders are on Guard

> Be on guard for yourselves and for all the flock, among which the Holy Spirit has made you overseers, to shepherd the church of God which He purchased with His own blood. I know that after my departure savage wolves will come in among you, not sparing the flock; and from among your own selves men will arise, speaking perverse things, to draw away the disciples after them.
>
> - Acts 20:28-30

In this particular passage, Paul calls the elders together and exhorts them to be on guard in three areas:

A. Guard Themselves

Effective elders watch themselves and guard their conduct and attitude first and foremost. Elders who are not seen as striving to grow and develop in personal spiritual maturity have no respect among the brethren and without respect they cannot be effective. The church will be patient and forgiving with an elder's weakness if he is striving to improve it. More elders lose their effectiveness because they mistakenly think that being an elder excuses them from having to deal with sinful habits and sinful character traits such as pride, laziness, gossip and worldliness.

B. Guard the Flock

Effective elders understand that once they become elders they have to change their priorities. Many times men take on the role of elder and see it as an extra duty, like a religious hobby that they add to their schedules. But eldership is like marriage, it changes your whole life and your schedule. The most effective elders are those that guard the flock 24/7, not just at Sunday and Wednesday services. You cannot be effective as a shepherd without being deeply involved in the lives of the sheep seven days a week.

C. Guard the Word

Note in Paul's encouragement and meeting with them that there was no talk of buildings, money or programs. These were matters that the deacons were concerned about. Effective elders concerned themselves with their ongoing personal spiritual development, the needs and direction of the spiritual lives of the members and the accurate teaching and preaching of God's Word. Effective eldering requires men who resist the temptation to do the more tangible work that belongs to deacons, and tackle the more challenging and demanding work of building the kingdom within the members!

The Word tells us that effective elders accept and excel in guarding themselves, the church and the Word against the world and against the forces of evil and darkness.

Habit #2 – Effective Elders are on Duty

This is a personal observation, but I have noticed that the most successful elders are the ones who carry the shepherd's staff wherever they go. In other words, their lives are defined by their role as elders in the church. You see it in the way they talk, the way they act and the way they react to things in or out of the church. Some elders are elders when they are in the building or at an elders' meeting. But effective elders are elders at ball games, picnics, work or wherever they are. No other role, whether it be their job or favorite hobby, is more emphatic than their role as elder. When they share with others that they serve as elders, people are not surprised.

Elders who are "on duty" realize that in this world there are many lost sheep looking for a shepherd and they have been ordained by God to find them wherever they are.

Habit #3 – Effective Elders are on Fire

> Now there were at Antioch, in the church that was *there*, prophets and teachers: Barnabas, and Simeon who was called Niger, and Lucius of Cyrene, and Manaen who had been brought up with Herod the tetrarch, and Saul. While they were ministering to the Lord and fasting, the Holy Spirit said, "Set apart for Me Barnabas and Saul for the work to which I have called them." Then, when they had fasted and prayed and laid their hands on them, they sent them away.
>
> - Acts 13:1-3
>
> Therefore, being sent on their way by the church, they were passing through both Phoenicia and Samaria, describing in detail the conversion of the Gentiles, and were bringing great joy to all the brethren. When they arrived at Jerusalem, they were received by the church and the apostles and the elders, and they reported all that God had done with them.
>
> - Acts 15:3-4

I list these passages in order to point out that elders (teachers) were involved in the great mission work of Paul to the Gentiles. For Jewish Christians it took great courage to encourage and support this type of activity among the Gentiles, but they were enthusiastic for the gospel.

So many times elderships are reduced to being decision making bodies that give the thumbs up or down for budget items, instead of being on the edge of launching new ideas and efforts to seek and save the lost as well as ministering to the saints. Elders that are "fired up" about evangelism or helping the poor or strengthening the church provide the kind of leadership people will follow. Effective elders lead by example, highly effective elders lead by inspiration, and inspiration is what leads the church to do great things for God.

Habit #4 – Effective Elders are on the Same Track

> ...with all humility and gentleness, with patience, showing forbearance to one another in love, being diligent to preserve the unity of the Spirit in the bond of peace.
>
> - Ephesians 4:2

Paul understood that when you take people who are divided by culture, social position, education, each with their own sinful flesh, and try to make one unified body out of these separate parts, you have to work at it! It is no different with elders and their efforts to work together as a unified group. Why do you think the qualifications for eldership stress those things that enable a man to get along with others? I Timothy 3:2-7 lists sixteen qualifications describing the elder candidate. Of these sixteen, eight refer to his ability to relate to other people, especially other elders because these are the men he will spend a lot of time with.

Effective elders are those who truly are temperate, prudent, hospitable, not addicted to wine (or anything for that matter), not confrontational, not argumentative, not self-willed ("got to have my way") not proud (cannot admit weakness or fault). Effective elders work on their relationships with each other. They invest time and effort into this for several reasons:

1. Causing division and conflict among the elders is always the first plan of attack for Satan.

2. Eldering is a "group task" not an individual task, so the more unified and team-oriented the eldership is, the more successful.

3. The church is a reflection of the eldership. A divided, do-nothing eldership will produce the same kind of congregation.

Effective elders recognize that a healthy, open, unified group of elders is Biblical in nature and a source of comfort and confidence to the congregation. We don't like to see our parents fight, we don't like to see our elders fight either.

They not only know this but they take concrete steps to maintain that unity of the Spirit, and work diligently at keeping the peace among themselves, and they do it for the love of Christ and the sheep He died to save.

Summary II

Obviously, so much more could be said about this very important subject, but these four will suffice. Effective eldering requires that these men be on guard each day for the spiritual well-being of themselves, the church and the teaching of the Word.

They need to be on fire in order to inspire the church with their zeal to serve the Lord, the church and the lost. If the elders don't inspire, who will? You cannot hire out inspiration.

Effective elders are also a force for unity, peace and reconciliation. This stands out in the leadership and as a result it permeates the entire congregation. Effective leadership in the church is the key to growth because the church cannot grow beyond its leadership.

I hope you will continue to pray and support your eldership as they seek to become more and more effective as each year goes by.

7 HABITS OF HIGHLY EFFECTIVE
DEACONS

In his book, *7 Habits of Highly Effective People*, Steven Covey reviews 200 years of literature devoted to success and human development and distills these into seven basic principles. His conclusion is that successful and effective people, regardless of the time and place they lived in, shared some common characteristics that enabled them to become highly effective as artists, politicians, business people, teachers and so on. In essence, he says that they were people who were motivated by principles rather than profit, people who worked at being something rather than having something.

Using Mr. Covey's approach, I have studied the Bible and used my experience in church work to identify some of the characteristics that make for successful Christian living and effective ministry as elders and ministers.

In this chapter I would like to close out the series with a lesson describing the seven habits of highly effective deacons.

Steven as a Model – Acts 6-7

The Bible does not list the qualities needed for being effective as a deacon, like Mr. Covey does in his book, but it does give us a model we can study.

A man named Stephen was one of the first to be chosen by the church and appointed by the Apostles to serve the church in a special way. Many see him as the template for service as a deacon. In looking at his life, we can determine the kind of habits necessary to become effective as a deacon.

A brief portrait of him is given in Acts 6 and 7

> Now at this time while the disciples were increasing in number, a complaint arose on the part of the Hellenistic Jews against the native Hebrews, because their widows were being overlooked in the daily serving of food. So the twelve summoned the congregation of the disciples and said, "It is not desirable for us to neglect the word of God in order to serve tables. Therefore, brethren, select from among you seven men of good reputation, full of the Spirit and of wisdom, whom we may put in charge of this task. But we will devote ourselves to prayer and to the ministry of the word." The statement found approval with the whole congregation; and they chose Stephen, a man full of faith and of the Holy Spirit,
>
> - Acts 6:1-5a

Habit #1 – Effective Deacons are Spiritually Minded

Stephen was a man who believed and in whose life the Spirit was at work. Being "full" of the Spirit means that the Spirit is producing much fruit (love, joy, peace, patience, etc.) in you. It also means that the Word of the Spirit is alive in you (you know and obey it). Jesus said in John 4:23 that God is looking for those who will worship Him in spirit and truth. We mistakenly think that so long as deacons know how to do tasks like carpentry or web-hosting they are qualified, but the Bible says that the first criteria, the first habit that should be evident in them is that they be spiritually minded men, men who truly believe, know and practice the words of Christ.

Habit #2 – Effective Deacons are Effective Workers

> The word of God kept on spreading; and the number of the disciples continued to increase greatly in Jerusalem, and a great many of the priests were becoming obedient to the faith.
>
> - Acts 6:7

Notice that the task of feeding the poor and widows is not mentioned again. What is mentioned, however, is the continued growth of the church, and along with that growth the probable increase in the need for ministry. Once the Apostles gave the task over to Stephen and the others, it was taken care of without further mention. This means that:

- The Apostles were free to minister the Word, pray and shepherd the church.
- The poor received the food they needed.
- The church continued to grow.

What was important to Stephen was the fact that the job was done and done right, not the fact that he was now a deacon. The task is what is important, not the title.

Deacons are the ones that do a lot of the "heavy lifting" in the church. This is the point of being a deacon. Deacons not only know how to serve, they want to serve and they are good at it because they have developed the habit of effective service.

Habit #3 – Effective Deacons Submit to Leadership

> And Stephen, full of grace and power, was performing great wonders and signs among the people.
>
> - Acts 6:8

Although Stephen was already a man of great faith and spirituality, he did not see his role as one to advise or conflict with his leaders. He had the support of the congregation but did not use this to divide the church or develop a following or influence. He was not one to form a clique or challenge the elders, he merely did his work and allowed God to work in him.

Effective deacons respect the leadership of other men, even though these men may be weak and sinful at times. A deacon's wisdom is demonstrated in his submission. Even when he could exercise miraculous powers, Stephen continued to serve and submit to the leadership of the Apostles.

Habit #4 – Effective Deacons Continually Develop Their Skills

> But some men from what was called the Synagogue of the Freedmen, including both Cyrenians and Alexandrians, and some from Cilicia and Asia, rose up and argued with Stephen. But they were unable to cope with the wisdom and the Spirit with which he was speaking.
>
> - Acts 6:9-10

Successful, effective deacons are always expanding their capacity to serve. Stephen, for example, began with the task of benevolence in food distribution, but he developed and used his other gifts as well. He used his gifts to evangelize and he used his wisdom to defend the faith.

Sometimes deacons think they are limited and can only do one thing, but in order to grow we must follow the pattern for growth which is relatively simple to explain. The pattern for personal growth in ministry is as follows:

A. Learn how to do the job yourself.

B. Teach someone else to do the job well.

C. Learn a new job.

D. Repeat the cycle.

This is how deacons grow, how they help the church to grow, and how they gain satisfaction from their work.

Habit #5 – Effective Deacons Take Criticism Well

> Then they secretly induced men to say, "We have heard him speak blasphemous words against Moses and against God." And they stirred up the people, the elders and the scribes, and they came up to him and dragged him away and brought him before the Council. They put forward false witnesses who said, "This man incessantly speaks against this holy place and the Law; for we have heard him say that this Nazarene, Jesus, will destroy this place and alter the customs which Moses handed down to us." And fixing their gaze on him, all who were sitting in the Council saw his face like the face of an angel.
>
> - Acts 6:11-15

Stephen's increased ability and ministry made him subject to attack. However, he was able to keep a sweet Christian spirit, even when unjust attacks were made against him. Anyone who has served the church knows that these kinds of attacks are the hardest of all to suffer. The ones we don't deserve are the ones that hurt the most.

Leadership of any kind is like that, it makes us visible, accountable and attackable. Deacons, and especially their wives, need to understand and accept this reality. The successful, effective deacon will be able to do his very best, be criticized for it, and still maintain his spiritual balance and enthusiasm.

Now we know that the successful deacon will have already cultivated this habit of weathering criticism because he will have already mastered this next habit even before being a deacon.

Habit #6 – Effective Deacons Study the Word

In this long passage Stephen, as he is brought before the religious leaders of his day, is able to defend the faith that he has. He reviews the history of the Jews and God's dealings with them. This summary demonstrates that Stephen knew God's Word and knew it well.

In front of his accusers he was able to explain what God really said and meant in His Word. This required Bible reading and study. He was strong in the Scriptures and this made him a powerful witness when the opportunity came.

Stephen demonstrates that Bible study and service are not mutually exclusive things. I served at a congregation once where several of the deacons would roam the halls during Bible class and then hang out in the foyer during the sermon so they could open the doors at the end of service. They thought that their "service" in putting up communion trays or door monitoring excused them from sitting through a class or a sermon.

Being a deacon, or doing the work of a deacon, is not some kind of "hall pass" to get you out of studying God's Word. As a matter of fact, knowing the Word well is what enables a deacon to do and serve in ways that are in accordance to God's will and thus become effective. You see, it is not just what you do, or how much you do that makes you an effective deacon, it is if you do it according to the spirit and will of God, and for this to happen, you need to know His Word.

Habit #7 – Effective Deacons Rely on God

> Now when they heard this, they were cut to the quick, and they began gnashing their teeth at him. But being full of the Holy Spirit, he gazed intently into heaven and saw the glory of God, and Jesus standing at the right hand of God; and he said, "Behold, I see the heavens opened up and the Son of Man standing at the right hand of God." But they cried out with a loud voice, and covered their ears and rushed at him with one impulse. When they had driven him out of the city, they began stoning him; and the witnesses laid aside their robes at the feet of a young man named Saul. They went on stoning Stephen as he called on the Lord and said, "Lord Jesus, receive my spirit!" Then falling on his knees, he cried out with a loud voice, "Lord, do not hold this sin against them!" Having said this, he fell asleep.
>
> - Acts 7:54-60

In his worst moment Stephen reveals the essential quality that made him an effective deacon, he relied totally on God. In everything he did, from serving food to preaching and debating which led to his witness of faith that cost him his life, Stephen was a man who sought after and depended on God. We need to understand that becoming a deacon has a double-edged quality to it: many times men are chosen for this role because they are talented, self-starters, successful, good organizers, etc. With time, however, we find out that these very qualities often lead these men to rely on themselves and their own skills or strength. The result is that these kinds of men often wait until they are in deep trouble before they will call on others or on God for help.

The highly effective deacon is a man who puts his talents, ability and resources into God's hands and depends wholeheartedly on the Lord to direct and support him in ministry.

Whether it is planting flowers, helping the poor, managing the budget or visiting and caring for the sick and dying, all things are done in the strength of the Lord and for His glory.

Summary

Isn't it amazing that it was not an Apostle or preacher or elder who was first martyred for Christ? It was a deacon! And isn't it amazing that the death of this deacon served as the catalyst for an evangelistic thrust that eventually brought one who supported his execution, Saul of Tarsus, to Christ?

The Bible says that deacons who serve well (meaning serve effectively) receive a high standing and have confidence in Christ (I Timothy 3:13). Stephen's life shows that he received both these things:

1. He received honor (high standing) because he had the privilege of giving up his entire life in one moment for the glory of Christ.

2. He had great confidence before death because God opened his eyes to see the kingdom of heaven, in heaven, and the Lord Himself there at the right hand of God. Stephen, like the Apostle John, saw all of this while still in his earthly body!

There is no guarantee that our deacons will not have to face death for Christ, and no promise that they will glimpse the heavenly realm while here on this earth, however, they do receive honor from the Lord in His Word for their service and are respected by the church for their special leadership role in ministry. In addition to this, they will have greater knowledge of and intimacy with the Lord as they grow to resemble Him more and more through their service in His name.

There are rewards for serving as a deacon and the wise deacon will pursue these through effective service.

I would like to take this opportunity to commend all deacons everywhere for their good work and exhort them to press forward in the search to be highly effective in their ministries.

This can be achieved by cultivating the habits I mentioned in this session:

- Spiritual mindedness
- Conscientious service
- Submission to leadership
- The ongoing development of skills
- A humble spirit in dealing with criticism
- A knowledge of God's Word
- An absolute trust in the Lord for all things

I hope that these habits will begin to describe your ministry and spirit as deacons as we all strive to serve the Lord with all our hearts, minds and strength. God bless you all in your ministries.

BibleTalk.tv is an Internet Mission Work.

We provide textual Bible teaching material on our website and mobile apps for free. We enable churches and individuals all over the world to have access to high quality Bible materials for personal growth, group study or for teaching in their classes.

The goal of this mission work is to spread the gospel to the greatest number of people using the latest technology available. For the first time in history it is becoming possible to preach the gospel to the entire world at once. BibleTalk.tv is an effort to preach the gospel to all nations every day until Jesus returns.

The Choctaw Church of Christ in Oklahoma City is the sponsoring congregation for this work and provides the recording facilities and oversight.

choctawsaints.org/support-bibletalk

BIBLETALK.TV

54075904R00026

Made in the USA
Lexington, KY
01 August 2016